FAMILY STORIES

My *father's parents in front of
their house in the Shtetel, about* 1928

FAMILY STORIES
TRAVELS BEYOND THE SHTETEL
by ROSE CHORON

WITH ILLUSTRATIONS FROM

Small Town, My Destroyed Home, A Recollection

by ISSACHAR BER RYBACK

Joseph Simon   Pangloss Press

Illustrations from Issachar Ber Ryback's series,
Shtetel Mayn Khoyever Heym, a Gedenknish
(Small Town, My Destroyed Home, A Recollection)
through the courtesy of the Israel Museum, Jerusalem.

Design by Joseph Simon

Library of Congress Cataloging-in-Publication Data

Choron, Rose,
   Family stories : travels beyond the shtetel / by Rose Choron ; with
illustrations from ''Small Town, My Destroyed Home, A Recollection'' by
Issachar Ber Ryback.
        p.   cm.
   ISBN 0–934710–17–1 : $17.50
     1. Jews—Lithuania—Social life and customs.   2. Choron, Rose.
            3. Lithuania—Social life and customs.   I. Ryback,
Issachar, 1897–1935.   II. Title.
DS135.R93L552   1989   88–38796
947'.5004924–do19   CIP

To my mother and father

The shoemaker

6

Speak in French when you can't think of the English for a thing—turn out your toes when you walk—and remember who you are!

Lewis Carroll—*Alice's Adventures in Wonderland*

The fish market

Contents

The knife sharpener

Illustrations

Preface

It was through my nephew Paul that I embarked upon my voyage into the past. He arrived one day with a recording machine. "Aunt Rose," he said, "you are the one who still remembers the olden days. Tell me about our family. What was my grandfather like? How did Jews live in Russia? Did you leave Germany before Hitler arrived?"

*My parents, father's parents, sister
and two nephews, about 1928*

13

I realized that he knew nothing about his origins. Nor did my other nephews and nieces. Instead of talking into Paul's cassette, I took to the pen. For quite a while I had been writing, but it so happened that of late the Muse had abandoned me. Now Paul's request sent me off again. I plunged into the past, and came up with this book.

I gave myself free rein, writing both on some of my own experiences and on the common background of family members and friends between and around World War I and World War II. With this in mind, I recall life in a Lithuanian *shtetel*, then in Berlin, Switzerland, and intermittently in other countries, including the United States and Israel. I have tried to convey the general climate and atmosphere of all these places at the time, as well as personal episodes. The stories are primarily about my own and other Jewish families

My *father with his youngest and oldest sister, plus seated family and nanny*

My mother with four children

migrating from the *shtetel* into the outside world. They tell about young people growing up under such circumstances, exposed to constant readjustments and dangers.

Thanks to my father's foresight, none of us suffered the dreadful fate of so many other Jews. As representative of an important chemical concern in Germany, he very soon became aware of the political developments, and did not rest until all members of our numerous clan, including uncles, aunts and cousins were safe.

Father was a warm-hearted, generous man with a great love and understanding for us children. He was also a wonderful story teller, I never tired of listening to him. The first story that now came into my mind, was "The Bundist." About his voyage to America, alone on a big freighter at the age of thirteen, and about his adventures in the new country.

"Trains" was the next story that occurred to me, drawing on one of my first and most traumatic childhood experiences.

One memory led to another. Throughout, I tried to retain my original feelings and impressions. Since then, of course, things have changed, and with them some of my perceptions.

This is true, for example, about Switzerland. We lived there for ten years before the War, and during all that time none of us ever set foot in a Swiss home. We were part of the Jewish community, and had no social contact with non-Jews. Much of this has changed. The Swiss now appear a more open community, if I am to judge from my own experiences.

I am the only Jew among farmers and vinegrowers in my small village near Lausanne. Like any one of them I tend my

My *father with parents and oldest and youngest brother*

My mother's father and mother

garden, pick plums and pears, water the flowers, put out the garbage, and shovel snow. They accept me while respecting my different identity. Some have become good friends, and, through my influence, have visited Israel to learn new ways of farming, to swim at Elath, or to visit the ancient sites, which, in different ways, are holy to all of us.

I think particularly, in relation to this book, of one very special friend who, alas, died a few years ago. Dr. Oscar Forel, though of old Swiss stock, developed some very close personal connections with the Jews. His father, the great August Forel, a social leader, scientist and psychiatrist, was a distinguished figure in his country, whose portrait now graces the Swiss thousand franc notes. August Forel would have, no doubt, considered it a dubious honor to symbolize big money. In spite of his great disappointment in the Russian revolution, he remained a most ardent socialist throughout his life. He

17

had no special feelings for the Jews, but his son, my friend Oscar, made up for this. He too was a psychiatrist, and founder of a prestigious clinic, but it is his wartime and post-war activities in helping the victims of Hitler that illustrate the broadening of Swiss horizons.

Throughout the War, Oscar Forel used his clinic to shelter members of the French resistance as well as Jewish escapees from Germany and France. At night he sent out guides across the border to help these people into Switzerland where he would hide them until he could provide papers needed for their safety. After the War, he and some colleagues set up centers all over the country to help children, surviving the Holocaust, locate their families or friends, or else to place them in foster homes.

Dr. Forel's relation to Israel was particularly warm. When I first met him in 1969, he lived in his mansion "Le Manoir" on Lake Geneva, in the village of St. Prex, in which he was a revered figure. His house was always full of guests. Once a year, in the summer, his youngest daughter and her family came to visit him for a month. She lived in Israel, married to an Iraqi Jew, and her two sons Giliad and Amir were the grandfather's delight. He tried to teach them French and table-manners. Instead, the whole *Manoir* resounded with colorful bits of Hebrew—*rega, b'vakasha, todah raba*—picked up by the Italian cook and Chi, a Chinese pianist friend and visitor.

I have spelled this out, as an unusual illustration of how Jewish life impinged on this tiny area of Switzerland after the War. It is not, for me, the only illustration. Though I now visit St. Prex with nostalgia since Dr. Forel's death, I sometimes stop to see one of his neighbors, a former president of

18

Switzerland, Hans Schaffner and his wife Ruth, bringing them cherries and greengage plums from my garden, and joining them in a glass of wine. They are great friends of Israel, and Mr. Schaffner, though non-Jewish, is interested in the Yiddish language, which he likes to compare with his native Schweizerdeutsch, trying to find affinities.

I live in my Swiss village most of the year, painting, writing, dreaming, attending to the garden and my house-guests, with intermittent trips to London, Zurich, and Israel. When fog and ice descend upon me, I take off for New York, to spend a few months visiting my family and friends, and to refuel my soul with concerts, plays, museums and lectures.

The United States, too, is not what it used to be when I first set eyes on the Statue of Liberty in 1939. How shocked I was

My father (second from right, with book)
with his family, about 1901

19

*My parents with four children and
mother's father, about* 1927

then, after I reached the shrine of "equal rights" and found
out about housing areas, clubs, and hotels that were restricted
—closed to Jews. It was common knowledge that there was a
numerus clausus in universities and private schools, and we
were told that Jews had no place in banks and basic industries.
Travelling through the country, I sometimes had to go far
out of my way to find an inn or room without a sign which
meant Jews not admitted.

Things are very different now, of course. Overt discrimination
is illegal, though painful manifestations of anti-Semitism still
exist like everywhere else in the world. Jews in America have
become prominent in almost every field. They are not neces-
sarily more popular, but they seem to have reached a different
standing. The universal sense of guilt after the Holocaust has
surely caused a change of attitude towards the Jews, and so
did the emergence of Israel. Whereas before, the Jew was
stereotyped as a stooped, frightened coward, he now is seen

as a strong soldier, upright, unafraid, able to win wars and stand up for his rights. For that he has earned general respect, yet still with reservations. If non-Jews can no longer despise the Jew for his old weaknesses, many, at present, accuse him of arrogance, especially concerning Israel. However, if in this sense Israel may sometimes lead to criticism, there can be no doubt that its existence has given Jews a new identity and independence. They now walk with their heads up.

All this is a long way from the simple stories in this book, and from the *shtetel* I look back to. No matter where I am now, and how much I outgrew its limitations, it still remains an undercurrent in my life. This is why I chose the beautiful drawings by Issachar Ber Ryback as illustrations. They are part of his book *"Small Town, My Destroyed Home, A Recollection,"* published in Berlin in 1923, and owned by the Israel

Father (on the right) *with his two younger brothers, and a friend* (seated) *about* 1925

Museum of Jerusalem, who gave us permission to reproduce them. Issachar Ber Ryback was born in 1897 in a small town, the *shtetel* of Elisabetgrad (now Kirovo). He studied at the Academy in Kiev, and learned a great deal from the French cubists and German expressionists. Most of his work relates to recollections of his youth and often reminds one of Chagall, though Ryback seems more tragic and more somber than his senior. The memory of his father, murdered in a pogrom, pursued him all his life. In 1926 he went to live in Paris, where he met with success. But on the eve of the opening of his large retrospective exhibition planned by the art dealer Wildenstein in 1935, he suddenly collapsed and died. He was thirty-eight years old.

His widow Sonia, helped to create and to run the Ryback house at Ramat Yosef in Israel. It is a small, delightful museum opened in 1962, to which Mrs. Ryback donated the entire collection of her husband's works, including his charming ceramic figures depicting types of the *shtetel*. In the spring of 1988, Ryback's prints and drawings were shown with those of Chagall and Lissitzky, among others, in an exhibition of Russian-Jewish avant-garde artists, first at the Israel Museum in Jerusalem, and later at the Jewish Museum in New York. Twenty-six are reproduced in this book, not in any order or direct relationship to the stories.

My friends have been very supportive throughout my excursion into the past, and I am grateful to them, particularly to Marie Lampard, Jerome Mazzaro, and Caroline Tumarkin, who listened and offered stimulating advice. Above all I feel fortunate to have encountered my publisher, Joseph Simon. His good taste and expertise have been most helpful in producing this book.

My *mother's father*

Evening

Escape

Three troikas sped in full moon
Through the crystal night,
Propelling powdered snow, bright bells, and children's voices,
Balloons of many colors floating overhead.

"Sing children, sing," the mothers urged
When someone was in sight.

Two horsemen coming from the opposite direction, stopped the
    caravan.
"What's this merry-making all about?" they shouted.
"We're going to a wedding," the children chirped,
Sprinkling them with confetti.
"A wedding, eh? Here we wage wars,
Fighting our arse off for the revolution, and you make weddings!"

"Let's have our own," the other soldier roared.
"What of it little wench? Come on, get out,
Let's have some fun together!"
He pointed at poor Mendel, his mother had dressed up as girl
To save him from the claws of the Red Army.

She held him tight under the blanket
And tears of terror choked her voice.
"Stop it," she screamed. "Don't touch her!
She's dying of consumption, can't you see?
She is contagious. That's why the others are in separate sleighs."

That did it. "Contagious, eh?" They stepped back horror-stricken.
"Go hang yourself with your damned daughter, you old bitch,"
  they swore.
"May you both burn in hell!"
With that, they crossed themselves, spat on the snow, and fled.

Never were curses taken with more glee.
Trembling all over, Gita hugged her son.
"I almost had a heart attack," she muttered to herself.

She closed her eyes while they resumed their journey.
It all came back to her as on a screen.

They had left home in Lithuania, the Germans on their heels,
And pitched their tents in Riga, awaiting to return after the war.
But soon the Bolsheviks invaded Latvia.
Gita's and Raya's husbands, merchants, considered capitalists,
Fled to Vienna, to make arrangements for their families to follow.

The Reds, at first, had just a voluntary army.
As civil war expanded, they introduced compulsory conscription,
And, one by one, Gita's four sons were called to serve.

She almost lost her mind.
For nothing in the world would she entrust her flesh and blood
To Russians, red or white: "once a pogromnik, always one!"
That was her own conviction and her sons'
Who would not risk their lives for Jew-baiters.

Her oldest, Saul, uncouth, half blind, with a wild mane and
    beard,
Was in no danger. They took one look at him, and sent him
    home.
David, her Hercules, however, had everything an army looked for:
Brains, muscles, endless energy.

Brooding in bed all night, Gita contrived a plan.
When David was called up, she cut Saul's hair and beard
Leaving a thin moustache, put his new glasses on him with
    black rims,
And sent him with his brother's orders in his stead.
The trick worked wonders. David was exempted.

Encouraged by success, Gita shaved Saul's moustache and head,
Gave him her husband's business suit, spats, top hat, tie,
And off he went, to play the part of Chaim,
Her dearest son the future doctor, just recruited.

For once roles were reversed,
And Saul took care of his more able brothers.
He was proud of his task and felt important.

This time things did not go so well.
Gita sat up all night in panic, waiting for her son,
Convinced that something dreadful had occurred.

Next morning he arrived, dishevelled and bewildered,
No spats, no tie, no hat. His outfit had created a sensation.
They laughed at him, called him a Jewish dandy,
Adjourned his medical examination,
Stuck him into the barracks overnight.
When finally Saul saw the doctor, his bad eyes paid off once
        again,
And, in Chaim's name, he was dismissed.

Gita's bluff had worn thin. She had to find another one for
        Mendel,
Her youngest, just turned eighteen, a blue-eyed dreamer and
        musician.

Meanwhile her bin was empty and the furnace frozen.
Her able-bodied sons were hiding in the cellar,
And Saul, her problem child, became the sole provider of the
        family.
He milked the cows and fed the chickens for a farmer,
In turn, brought home milk, eggs, and bread.

Gita, a cheerful matron, dark and plump,
Had a kind word and smile for everyone.
She liked to cook, to eat, to give.

Now she had shrunk to half her size, starving on beets and
   cabbage,
To supplement meals of her pregnant sister Raya and five
   children,
With her own rations.
Though she was worn and tired, her eyes kept sparkling,
Spurring the spirits of the others.
Trust in their husbands' wits and efforts kept the sisters going.
They waited anxiously for news, bags packed, ready to leave.

The day Mendel received his military orders,
An older man in overalls and lumber-jacket,
Sparing of words, efficient and discreet,
Arrived from Vienna, and took over.

Otto appeared at night with three big troikas
Filled with straw, and pulled by husky horses.
While neighbors were in bed and Raya's children sleeping,
In silence, not to draw attention, they packed all trunks
Under the straw on which they were to sit.

Mendel, in a blond wig, green velvet cape and hood,
Sat next to Gita in the leading troika,
With Otto as their coachman.
Under their seat, David and Chaim were hiding in the straw.

When this first sleigh was ready, waiting in the dark,
Raya woke up her brood.
She kept the little ones with her in the next troika,
And in the last one were the other three with Saul.

The children had been told
That they were going to a wedding in the country.
Cheering and unaware of hazards, they sang and laughed
Against the bitter cold that blew through straw and blankets.
Unwittingly, they gave the dangerous expedition
The casual face it needed for its ploy.

After she fended off Mendel's fierce suitors,
Gita fell fast asleep, wrapped in her fur.
Otto's voice from the box-seat woke her:
"Get ready, we are almost there!"

In a flash she perked up. This was the crucial moment.
Once her three military rebels and deserters
Left red Latvia undetected, they all were safe.
For the time being there was peace at home in Lithuania.
The year was 1919, The Germans had evacuated. The Reds had
        not yet come.

They reached the border at three in the morning, just as planned.
The customs clerk came out into the cold, dragging his feet.
"Where is your luggage," he asked, yawning.
"We have none," Gita answered with conviction.
"We're going to a wedding, and coming back tomorrow night."

He took their papers upside down, and stamped them.
"God bless you," he mumbled, half asleep.
Then, suddenly, he caught himself.
Raising his fist he shouted: "Long live Lenin,"
And let them pass.

The band

Folk Song

The radio turns me yesterwards
With an old Yiddish song.

My mother hums it.
Apron-covered, kerchief-coiffed,
She rolls out dough
On a worn, wooden board.

Behind the kitchen window
Snow flakes dance their jig.
With tom-cat Mishka on my lap,
I snuggle up to the tiled oven.
Its belly bears
Baked braided bread
To welcome the Sabbath.

I purr in unison with Mishka,
Beguiled by blind belief
In the benevolence of
God and man.

The News thwarts my idyllic vision.

Synagogue street

The Bundist

In the fall of 1905, my father at thirteen,
Was wanted by the Czar's police,
As member of the Jewish socialist *Bund*.

His parents whisked him off to Bremen overnight,
And sent him on a freighter to America.
Around his neck he wore a tag with the address
Of uncle Joseph in Reading, Pennsylvania.

The telegram announcing his arrival went astray.
When two weeks later he landed in New York,
There was no one to meet him.

He found his way to Reading, and coming off the train,
Spotted an Ice Cream sign above a shop window.
He took it for a Jewish name,
Pronounced Itze Cram.

The shop belonged to an Irishman.
But a Jewish customer, a junk dealer, spoke Yiddish.
He offered him a cone, and took him on his cart
To uncle Joseph's haberdashery.

His uncle did not welcome him with wine and *lekach*.
Without delay he set him down to work.

For a cot in the cellar and a pauper's pay,
The boy slaved all winter from four in the morning
Till late at night.

He kept the furnace going, scrubbed floors,
Charmed clients, dealers, took care of deliveries.
But he ate in the kitchen with the servants,
Receiving no kind word, lest he ask for a raise.

By spring he knew the language and the trade.
With savings he bought ties, belts, garters and a peddler's tray,
And took himself off to New York without good-byes.

There he peddled his way from door to door.
For ten cents a night he slept in dormitories
With Bowery bums as bed-fellows,
And for the price of a beer, the pubs offered
Chips, pickles, pretzels, nuts,
Of which he made his meals.

When winter came, freezing, undernourished,
He caught pneumonia, fainted in the street,
And, picked up by police, he was returned to Reading.

The uncle had spent sleepless nights
After the disappearance of his brother's son
And loss of his best worker.

This time he greeted him with open arms
And nursed him back to health.
A contract guaranteed good pay and normal hours,
And he was graciously admitted to the table.

Hard-working, bright, and trustworthy,
He grew to be his uncle's mainstay.

But lonely for his family, the *shtetel*,
And a sweetheart he had left behind,
He soon decided to go home.

Two years before, he had set out a revolutionary *Gymnasiast*,
A bundle on his back, a tag around his neck.
He now returned in a bright checkered suit,
White pointed shoes and tilted straw hat.

Loaded with gifts and new American speech and sparkle,
He tap-danced off the boat, took a deep breath,
And in full voice gave forth the song of
"Yankee Doodle," who, too, had come to town.

---

*lekach, honey cake; *Gymnasiast*, high school student.

The mother-in-law

Trains

Russia had lost a war and won a revolution.
The Balts regained their independence,
And all my family returned from Russian exile
Home to Lithuania.

We travelled on a cattle train,
Side by side with a pullman repatriating officers
And their families.
Both trains kept the same schedule,
Ignored all stations, and stopped at random
In fields and woods.

A twelve hour trip took twelve days.
Sitting on flea-infested straw,
I clung to mother's skirts,
Still shocked by memories of war.

A little girl my age was on the other train.
Her carriage always held in front of ours.
I watched her open-mouthed.
An apparition from another world.
Never had I seen a child
As groomed, grown-up and independent.

Red locks were tied back with black taffeta ribbons,
She wore white sparkling dresses
Under a pink pinafore,
A long silk scarf around her neck to keep her warm,
And her bright patent-leather shoes were mirrors.

At each halt she climbed down alone,
Sat on the grass and played with dolls,
While I watched longingly.
When whistles blew to call us back,
She clambered up the steps all by herself.

I often saw her with her father,
Standing at their window.
In uniform bedecked with medals,
He seemed so proud of his reconquered country.
But what a price he paid for it!

One day the whistle blew.
His daughter tried to mount the train
While it was moving.
Her scarf, caught in the wheels, pulled her under.

Holding on to my mother,
I screamed.

The girl was buried without ceremony,
And in deep silence we resumed our journey.

Our trains stopped twice a day to feed and air us.
Mother and I fetched water from a near-by well,
Crossing the rails between the high, forbidding wheels.
On open fire we cooked our daily brew
With turnips and potatoes,
Dreaming at night of savory roasts.

At last we reached the border and our *shtetel*.
Mother's brother stood at the station.
He came to fetch us with his horse and buggy,
A string of bagels around his neck.

Hugging and kissing, we ate him up, bagels and all.
Finally home, we threw ourselves upon the food awaiting us.
Never had chicken soup been such a treat.

But nothing matched the miracle
Of telephones, electric lights and flushing toilets.
The Germans had installed it all during their occupation,
Convinced that Lithuania would be theirs for good.

Our odyssey was over.
We slept in our clean sheets again.
For years the girl in the pink pinafore disturbed my nights.
But now, in haunted dreams, I see those other cattle trains.

The *wedding canopy*

Scribbler
on the Roof

Mother and father married
Against the wish of their parents:
She had no dowry and he no *tefillin*.
But love prevailed.

His father was the "Rothschild" of the *shtetel*, der *Gewir*,
Her's was its rabbi.
One dealt with *sechoyre*, the other with *Toyre*.

Both fled the German siege of Lithuania
During World War I,
And took their families to Russia.
The whole *kehille* cheered and danced at their return.

Our family *yches* was a burden for us children.
We had to set an example,
And being virtuous did not come naturally.

Father, for instance, when abroad on business,
Always came home loaded with toys.
In no time the village youngsters grabbed and smashed them.
Ready to kill, we screamed for our possessions.
But: "No! You have enough, and they are poor!
You must not shame them or provoke their envy!
Father will bring new toys next time."

He used to arrive in an automobile.
Our *shtetel* had never seen one before.

Adults and children came running
And called it a *golem*.

Thus private events became public domain.
A father, for instance, once caught his son
Scribbling a note on a Saturday.
To write on Shabbes! What a terrible sin!
The boy climbed on top of the roof,
And threatened to jump if punished.
Half the village assembled
To plead with him and bargain,
Till he deigned to repent,
And was spared public spanking.

At weddings brides and mothers drowned in tears.
To the tune of a fidgety fiddler,
The groom's friends danced
And carried him upon their shoulders,
While onlookers sang, clapping to the rhythm.

Our *shtetel* was rambling and ingrown,
Warped, thatch-roofed houses sprawling in wild gardens.
A mossy pine wood huddled up to it,
Its carpet strewn with blueberries,
Our treat after a dip in the cool brook.

Market days assembled *Yidden* and *Goyim*
On the dusty, swarming village square.
Beggars displayed maimed children to draw tears and alms.
Jugglers performed tricks for spellbound spectators,
And bead-bedecked gypsies foretold gloom and glory
From palms and tea leaves.
Behind their stalls, peasant girls, rosy, kerchiefed,
Showed off embroidered blouses, home-spun linens, woven
    baskets.

Farmers offered dry goods and greens,
Potatoes, onions, pears, and cherries.
They traded chickens, horses, sheep, pigs, cows.

We too had a cow.
She buttered our homemade bread and gave us cream and cheese,
And with our generous garden and egg-happy hens,
We did not feather the grocer's nest.

There was no running water.
The *mikve* kept us clean,
And a deaf and dumb village fool
Carried the drinking water from our own well.

The *Toyre* was supreme.
Everything turned around its study and interpretation.
The Book was the Law.
Queen of the week was *Shabbes*.
Holidays crowned the rest of the year.
Then Mother's kitchen bustled and buzzed long in advance.
The house was scrubbed and so were we.

Poor people starved themselves for the Holy Days,
And no matter how little they had,
There was always a piece of *challe* and a plate of chicken soup
For needy and lonely guests.

My *shtetel* has filled me with cheerful images,
But to spite Chagall,
Our cow would not fly.

---

tefillin, phylacteries; *Gewir*, leading citizen; *sechoyre*, goods; *Toyre*,
Torah; *kehille*, congregation; *yches*, important lineage; *golem*,
legendary robot come to life; *mikve*, ritual bath; *challe*, holiday plaited
bread.

The goat

The Cat

The whole house hummed, welcoming new-born Jonathan,
Except for Vassya, the fat, furry cat.

Crouched in a corner, dethroned and offended,
He refused to eat. Apologetically and in vain,
Malka cajoled him, offering liver, heavy cream.

But Friday was no time for sulking cats.
Malka got ready for Sabbath, her house all scrubbed,
The table set with candles, wine, and bread.
Her pots were steaming in the kitchen,
Keeping her busy with the festive meal,
While Jonathan slept quietly on the porch.

When she came out to see him,
A fluffy fur covered the crib,
Triumphantly and purring with delight.

"It's feeding time," said Malka, opening her blouse.
She took her baby from the crib and screamed.
The weight of the big cat had smothered him.

His father, coming home with Teddy-bear and tulips,
Was calling from downstairs "Shabbath Shalom!"

47

The *funeral*

Babushka

"Don't take away my grandmother," I screamed
And hit the strangers carrying her off.

Marussia picked me up in her strong arms.
She was the *niania* mother had engaged
To spend the summer with us on our *datsha*.
"Don't cry my darling," she tried to appease me,
"Babushka is in heaven watching over you.
She's sad to see you cry."

All week the house was full of people come
With cooked meals, cakes, nuts, fruit,
To pay condolences to Grandfather, their rabbi, and his children,
Crouched barefoot on low stools, as is the custom,
Mother lost in a corner, tears running down her cheeks.

No matter what Marussia told me,
I knew that something terrible had happened.
My sweet beloved Babushka was gone.
Dear Babushka who told us stories, sang lullabies while rocking
     us to sleep.

I sobbed and sobbed into Marussia's bosom, craving a caress.
Annoyed she carried me into the garden.
"Stop it" she scolded, "we all must die some day. That is the
    way of things.
If you are a good girl, you too will go to heaven."
This really got me.
I started up, jumped to the ground and stamped my foot:
"I do not want to go to heaven. No one will make me. I'll stay
    right here!"
I beat her with my fists and yelled "I'll never die. You are a
    liar, you are bad."

Marussia's patience had its limits. So did her peasant wisdom.
"It's you who are a bad girl," she yelled back.
"You will not go to heaven. You will go to hell."
With that she flung herself into the house, and left me to my lot.

Without a moment's hesitation, I turned around,
And running for my life, I dashed into the nearby woods.

Majestic pine trees sent forth soothing scents
To welcome me into their shrine.
I knew the forest well and felt at home.
The parents took us there for picnics, berries, dips into the brook.
Tired and bewildered, I cried myself to sleep on the soft mossy
    carpet.

Babushka came to comfort me.
She held me in her arms, and promised I would never die.
I woke with the sun setting, calm and reconciled.

When I arrived at home, my father was about to call the village
    guard.
I had been lost for hours. Mother was beside herself.
She spanked and hugged me all at once.
I hollered, but deep down I felt content and reassured.
Like Babushka, I had been gone. Like her, Mother had missed
    and mourned me.

For years I stood my ground,
Convinced that with strong will and vigilance
I would be in control of my own life, exist for ever.

One day I stumbled on my way to school,
And fainted from the pain of a sprained ankle.
When I came to, I found myself next to a stranger on a bench,
Not knowing how I got there.

I had passed out, bereft of my own will,
And been picked up and carried off like Babushka.

For the first time I realized my limits.
I bowed to higher power, and to Marussia, no more with us,
And pursued immortality on a more modest scale.

---

*niania, Russian nanny; *datsha*, Russian country home.

Blessing the candles

my flesh and blood

a cow is in my room.
she stands in a far corner
quiet undemanding
as if apologizing
for the imposition.
I realize that I forgot
to feed her.
she must be hungry.

but my bin is bare
two meager veal chops
and a mug of milk.
she gulps it all
and looks at me
with grateful trusting eyes.
I know the food is wrong
in quantity and kind.

she swallows
her own flesh and blood.
but can I give more than I have?
she should be on a farm
get proper care
while I would come to visit.
yet I can't part with her.
I love her.

she's my flesh and blood
so good and true
giving forgiving
oh so wise.
I put my arms around her
feel her warmth
and waking to bright cow-bells
turn off the alarm.

On a hot day

Scenes from Berlin

Leaving our *shtetel* for Berlin
Was a move to another planet.

Already on arrival
We had our first surprise: artichokes.
Mother had never seen this prickly cactus.
Convinced that it was fodder for the pigs
And an antisemitic joke,
She angrily rang for the waiter.

In came the chamber maid, a girl of eighteen.
She laughed and gently introduced us
To the outlandish dish.

Her name was Anni and she came from Berne.
The Swiss German she spoke resembled our Yiddish,
And she seemed no surprise.
We all took to each other,
And when we rented our own flat,
She came along as guardian angel.

Our studies were my mother's chief concern.
Anxious to give us all that she had missed,
The benefits derived of formal education,
She got us going before we walked.

Fluent, at five, in Russian, Yiddish, Lithuanian,
I went with children one year older, to a Jewish school
Where we were taught in German to speak Hebrew.

All at sea, I drowned in a confusion
Of languages and disasters.

Our guardian angel put ham on my bread,
The kosher teacher fell into a fit.
I hungrily hid in the loo to eat it,
Breaching the sacred laws of etiquette.

In utter innocence I provoked constant indignation,
And finally was switched to public school.

There the brute cane was king.
At each mistake we had to bare our bottoms,
To have rote knowledge flogged into us.
Not why and how but who and when was the question.

Mother had great respect for German education
And thought these hardships to be harsh
But necessary labor-pains of learning.

She was incapable of hurting anyone.
Extending her big heart, she remained unaffected
In the mundane and often mordant world
Of father's business circles, blushing for those
Who lied or paid false compliments.
Although shy and reserved, she tackled tasks efficiently,
Be it with drill and hammer, needle, broom, or spade.

When a young girl, and after graduating as a midwife,
She went into the villages delivering babies.

It was unusual for a rabbi's daughter to have a profession.
But with his meager salary, her father fed the poor.
There was but little left to nourish his own family,
And she felt it her duty to help out.

The work left her no time for further studies.
Yet, with her common sense and peasant intuition,
A perfect memory and gift for figures,
She stood well-grounded on her feet.

Many a time, in her quiet, unassuming way,
She caught my father in an error,
And rarely would he venture a decision without consulting her.

Uprooted, though, from home and from traditions,
Her own self-confidence was shaken,
And thereby her authority with us.
We felt her insecurity and did not trust her judgment.

Ashamed, for instance, of her Yiddish,
Mocked and disdained as bastard German,
We were ashamed for being ashamed.
Often our tantrums were disguised appeals
For sympathy and understanding.
But she was too constrained to talk things out
With just a smile, a kiss, a hug.

Only much later, after father died,
When she lived in Jerusalem with her own people,
Did she reveal to me the difficulties she had suffered.
Old, almost blind, she came to be my baby,
And we were able to exchange our love and our affection.

⟡

Now, thrown into the whirlpool of Berlin,
Mother managed to keep her head above water.

We were three children, with two more to come,
And our new house was a big, buzzing hive.

This sunny villa in the elegant Westend of Berlin,
Bought ready with its Persian rugs and baroque furniture,
Stood in a rose garden with trees,
Surrounded by jasmine and lilacs.

We planted parsley, dill and cucumbers,
And picked peaches and plums
To fill the fruit bowl on our table,
Set every day from morn to night
For friends and relatives to drop in at all hours.
By then I spoke Berliner German fluently, longing to belong.
But we were still outsiders,
"Juden" to the Germans, "Ostjuden" to German Jews.

⟡

One day a couple and their daughter
Stopped over for a week
On their way back to Soviet Russia.

Father's friend was a socialist of the old guard.
A true idealist, he quit his job in Germany
To serve humanity and help to build
A better world in his own country.

I spent eight blissful days with Olga,
My kind, my age, and speaking my own language,
And when they left, I cried real tears of grief.

A few months later, father came home
At an unusual hour, his face ashen and drawn,
With news about his friend.

He had been put to death for harboring "dangerous" plans,
His wife had lost her mind. Olga had vanished,
Roaming the streets, no doubt,
Like thousands of abandoned children
Called *narodniki*, the people's kin,
Who slept in stations, ruins, churches,
Rummaging garbage cans for food.

One day, after a concert, mother spotted Soniatshka,
Her long-lost cousin, given up for dead.

The Russian revolution had destroyed her family and fortune,
And now she barely lived by giving piano lessons.
Too proud, she declined all financial help;
So mother bought a Steinway grand
And all of us had to take lessons,
Including Anni and the cook.

But Soniatshka was much too gentle.
She could not master our unruly brood.

Mother promptly enrolled us in a music school.
David and Sam took up the violin and I, the piano,
While Soniatshka remained to supervise our homework.

When she got married to her childhood friend from Libau,
They moved into our upper story, turned a flat.

Mother was very fond of them. They belonged to her world
And helped her take care of us.

We loved their tomcat Pushkin, with whom we shared our meals,
The books they bought and games we played together.
They took us to the zoo, to concerts and to puppet shows,
To silent movies and museums.

We were too young to share
In what Berlin in its great twenties had to offer.
Names like Brecht, Reinhardt, Schoenberg, and the Bauhaus
Were vague notions, which only later acquired significance.

Our vicarious link with this exciting world
Was mother's nephew from South Africa.
He stayed with us and studied medicine.

A young man-about-town, he brought home spicy news and
     gossip.
We loved him like an older brother,
Until one day he cursed ''those dirty niggers''
Living in his country.

The only black we knew, the moor in *Struwelpeter*,
Was the most winning character in the whole book.

To hate someone just for his color made no sense.
It was a shock to our innocence, and unforgivable.

That was the end of "brother" Yan.
We put glue on his chair, frogs under his pillow,
Iodine into his coffee,
And he packed up for other quarters.

Meanwhile, tucked twice a week into the big Mercedes,
We were dispatched to our music lessons.

Despite her name, my teacher Fräulein Nibelungen
Was no Teutonic goddess. In fact, we were great friends.
She played the pieces for me, I played them back by ear,
And though I was her "Wunderkind," I still can't read a note.

Poor little Sam was much too young.
He wet his pants and cried, till finally we left him home.
But David was in love with his spirited Fräulein Schwarz.
She sowed the seeds of his passion for music.

Hidden behind the sofa, tears running down my cheeks,
I listened to him play.

Outwardly tomboy, I actually was shy.
Only with father did I show unrestrained feelings.
Curled up on his lap, I would devour his stories
About the pranks he used to play and his adventures.
He never preached, and understood all things
With humor and compassion.

His work kept him abroad much of the time,
And I missed him.

He was a self-made man
With sparkling eyes and wit
To kindle any heart.
Though he had little time for fun and recreation,
He loved life, dancing, singing, spectacles, good food.

When he invited businessmen and friends,
Our house would burst with Eastern hospitality.
To mother, guests were gods, and her home was their altar.

Our table groaned under the load of offerings,
Caviar, borscht, piroshkis, blinis, *kulibiak*,
Competing with gefillte fish, chopped liver, lox and bagels,
All savories exotic to the German palates,
While vodka and champagne were spurring spirits.

Father's two bachelor brothers came with friends,
Beautiful actresses, artists, writers.
Musicians played on balalaikas,
And a young aunt sang Russian folk songs and romances.

The Germans wallowed in wine and nostalgia,
Forgetting for a while,
That Jews were the cause of all evil.

It was the spring of 1929,
And Hitler had already shown his teeth.
Father dreaded their lethal bite.

He had experienced the upheavals of the Russian revolution
And was not going to await Messiah.
One morning he woke up and knew
That it was time to go.
Soniatshka had already left for Palestine,
With our Steinway to sustain her.

We packed our bags, locked up the house,
Made for the land of milk and money,
Where cows rang bells to welcome us.

---

kulibiak, Russian meat, fish, or cabbage pie.

Synagogue

Swiss Transit

The world, at first, laughed off the warnings of *Mein Kampf*
As passing frenzies. My father did not laugh.
Instead, he moved our tents from Berlin to Lausanne.

Ice-capped in the beginning, like their mountains,
The Swiss warmed up to us
After we paid our bills and kept to ourselves.

Mother appreciated their unpretentiousness,
And the appeal was mutual.
We settled in a rambling groundfloor flat
With sunny terraces and garden and felt at home.

In Germany, most anxious to fit in,
We Lithuanian children had turned into Prussian brats,
Outdoing the authentic ones in arrogance and toughness.

This left our new Helvetian pals untouched.
They laughed and nicknamed us "les boches," the Huns.

With Hitler on the scene,
We soon dropped "Deutschland Uber Alles."
Embracing our new homeland with conviction,
We sang its national anthem, yodelled, ate fondue,
Spoke French and Schwizerdütsch,
And felt more Swiss than Wilhelm Tell.

My sister Feny, still a baby, was at home,
And Rachel started elementary school.
David and Sam joined the Ecole Nouvelle.

Among their classmates in this private school
Were Mohamed Reza Pahlavi, future shah of Persia,
And his brother, as well as the crown-prince of Siam.

Once, in a fit of temper and gratuitously,
Mohamed bade his brother to stand still,
And hit his face until it bled.

The class dragged the prospective monarch
To the cellar and paid him back in kind.
At heart, the dean approved his boys' reaction,
But to avoid a diplomatic scandal, they were punished.

Mohamed was transferred to Le Rosey,
A snobbish institute catering to names and money.

In contrast, Siam's prince
Composed and staged light musicals
And was the darling of his friends and teachers.

All children but myself had found their proper niche.
I was an adolescent, hard to handle.

A Jewish boarding school was recommended.
Although I was much younger than the other girls,
My mother sent me to it "faute de mieux."

The head of La Ramée, "Madame" to all of us,
Held our reins with strong but gentle hands.
I liked her right away. Accepting her authority,
I felt secure.

For once I was the youngest, mothered and cajoled,
With someone always there to answer and explain.

We were twenty-five girls from all parts of the world.
Most had completed school, now wishing to learn French.
The Germans, though, were escapees from Hitler,
Their parents looking for new roots abroad.

I was the only one who went to the lycée in town,
Spending the week in La Ramée, week-ends at home.

Sometimes on Sundays, mother asked the girls for tea.
She made them feel at ease
And they all called her "Mutti," as we did.

Madame had grown to be a good friend of the family.
Through her, our house became a refuge for lost parents
She sent to father for advice and help.

In due time, Mutti had acquired a Chevy.
Her driving teacher was Sérai, a wiry, hawk-nosed Greek,
Well-mannered and of many talents.

His love affair with the Greek consul's wife
Had stirred the tongues of gossipmongers.

Disowned by his shocked parents,
He stopped his legal studies and looked for work.
Mutti engaged him as our tutor.

A racy stallion, dark, young, whimsical,
He was more pal than teacher, and the boys adored him.
Excellent at all sports, he launched us
Into tennis, ping-pong, bob-sledding and skiing.

On weekends and vacations we took to the mountains.
We hiked and picnicked, entered competitions,
Sometimes, alas, returning with limbs broken.

However little he had taught us otherwise,
Sérai blew a fresh, frisky wind into our sails.

Constantly in and out of feminine webs,
He finally got caught by a buxom Brunhild.
She brought a dowry of nine cats
And bore him two blond Goths.

Mutti, by now a fervent driver,
Took us for casual rides
Over high mountain peaks and valleys.

Sometimes we all went to Montreux to see her friends,
A family like us of Lithuanian origin.

With numerous relatives and neighbors,
They formed a *shtetel* within town, including
Shadchens, shnorrers, shtibel, and *yeshive,*
As well as open homes with *kreplach* soup and *latkes.*

Their only goal during these years
Was to keep constant contact
With the Jews in Germany and Poland,
Trying to get them out at any cost.

The secret links they had
With clergy and with governments abroad,
Enabled them to rescue many lives.

They even risked their own, forging passports and visas
And often smuggling escapees alone across the borders.
For bribing frontier-guards and the police,
Some, caught by Swiss authorities, were jailed.

On weekends, when our maid was off,
They used to send us fugitives to hide.
These people had arrived illegally,
And needed a safe roof and rest
Before continuing their journeys.

Some, though my age in years,
Had skipped whole generations overnight.
Their eyes mirrored the horrors they had seen,
And often in the morning, sheets were wet with tears.

---

*shadchens, matchmakers; shnorrers, professional beggars; shtibel, small prayer room; yeshive, Jewish study academy.

I*n the market*

village
happening

flames were consuming
an alpine farm
while silent crowds looked on
and waited for the fire brigade

the voluntary crew of peasants
dropped their ploughs
but first ran home
to dress for the occasion

when they arrived
to get the water going
in red-piped pale-blue uniforms
still buttoning up
adjusting belts and berets
as for a fashion show
the barns had merrily burned down

the owners stood perplexed
but spectators entranced
by the flamboyant sight
cheered their unproven heroes
friends husbands brothers sons

only the band was missing

After Succot

Interludes

After completing the lycée,
I went to London to improve my English.

There were no foreigners in school
But I and a young girl called Sarah,
Adopted daughter of Kemal Pasha.

She was the sister of his mistress Ulkü,
Whose pictures as a pilot, tennis champion,
And the star of Turkey,
Graced all its posters, magazines, and walls
To propagate the ideal of the liberated woman.
Sarah, her opposite, a frightened little mouse,
Was sent to finish school in London,
Without an inkling of the English language.

Only with me could she speak French.
Homesick and lost, she followed me like my own shadow.

Above all, she longed to return to Turkey.
This, without a diploma, would have been desertion.
Kemal Pasha despised all failure,
And she was terrified of him.

Meanwhile, with London's cold and fog
And only fireplaces for heat,
I caught pneumonia and flew home.

Sarah was panic stricken.
She had no other crutch than me.
Though she was two years older,
I felt I was forsaking a small child.

We had invited her to celebrate the new year
With us in the mountains.
But barely settled home,
I spotted a brief note in a Swiss paper:
On her way back to Turkey,
Sarah had "fallen" from the train and died.

The following summer I was asked
To join my friend Maria on a trip to Budapest.
When we arrived, the stairs of the hotel
Were laid out with red carpets.
A cheering crowd showered us with confetti.
"Here comes the harem of His majesty," they laughed.
Bewildered by this strange reception,
We pushed our way inside, and there we learned
That they were waiting for the Prince of Wales.

For reasons of security his floor was emptied of all guests,
Except for us, two harmless girls.

The prince arrived with a large retinue,
Accompanied by Wallis Simpson.
She wore her hair pulled back into a bun,
Man-tailored suits and shoes,
No makeup and no jewelry.

All afternoon they played cards in the bar,
The prince flushed, high with liquor,
And at the crack of dawn he woke us up,
Back from nightly orgies, drunk and boisterous.

Budapest seethed with paprika-spiced gossip.
Journalists had a feast.

When later, Wallis Simpson the new duchess
Appeared in *Vogue*, bejewelled, with curls and frills,
It all seemed a real masquerade.

Plunging, meanwhile, into the bubbly Magyar city,
We let ourselves be carried on its waves.
Gypsies played into our ears,
We danced the czardas and drank Tokay,
Went riding on a *pusta*, shooting ducks,
Explored the "Altstadt," sailed along the Danube,
Ate goulash, strudel, *kaiserschmarren*.

Streets and cafés were packed
With pleasure-seeking masses,
Grabbing it all before the storm broke loose.

From Budapest the train took me to Paris,
In time to get enrolled at the Sorbonne.

Now looking back, I realize that I was primed for change
From carefree girlhood into a world
Of fears, responsibilities and threats.

Switzerland, stern, self-protective,
Behind high mountains, secret bank accounts,
Its towns and villages geranium-clad and scrubbed,
Rich orchards, corn fields, vineyard tended lovingly,
The sound of cow bells in the distance,
Mutti and Father watching over us,
All this, a past illusion of stability and peace,
Shaken by tremors of reality.

Hitler's sword hung over Europe.
The war in Spain was raging,
With many friends involved.
Picasso painted "Guernica."
The World's Fair staged its dance macabre.
Paris was overrun by refugees,
All queuing for a permit
To stay, to work, to breathe,
The coveted "laisser passer,"
Misnamed by many a "laisser pisser."

I studied history of art and spent my days
In class and at the Louvre,
Or visiting old castles and cathedrals.

At night, with friends in a bistro,
We watched the sun set over Paris,
Looking for sparks of hope on the horizon.

With Europe in eruption,
Young people had no base on which to build.

My brothers left to study in the States,
And in May 1939, we too folded our tents
And followed them.

Two weeks before we sailed,
I broke an ankle skiing
And boarded ship on crutches,
Leaning against real wood,
With but one leg to stand on.

When New York's diamond skyline
Gradually shone through the mist,
I felt its generous heartbeat
Long before we landed,
Throbbing in harmony with mine.

A heavy fog had lifted
And dispersed our Old World gloom.

Awe-stricken and in tears,
I hobbled off the boat
Onto the continent of open doors,
And limpingly, I made a go of it.

---

*pusta, Hungarian farm estate; kaiserschmarren, Austrian sweet dumplings.

I*n the living room*

My Sister Feny

This is where
I can rest my head,
Spill tears,
Throw off
Brassiere and girdle,
Lay bare blemishes,
Yet be held dear
For dimples and
In spite of warts.

We've waltzed at weddings,
Wept at wakes together,
Fought feuds
With kitten-paws.

There is a steady glow
In our hearth
No threatening flame.

Rejoicing in the Law

The Oak and The Willow

One night my uncle Joshel was arrested.
"Illegal speculation" they called his offense,
And shipped him, with eight others from his *shtetel*, to Siberia.

There they were put to work on hydroelectric dams,
Yevgeny Yevtushenko's *"temples of kilowatts."*

Such power-stations, offsprings of its industrial expansion,
Shot up all over Russia after the revolution.

Men stood for hours in ice water to erect them, frozen,
    undernourished.
They were inmates of labor camps. Most died within a year,
Replaced immediately by new men, picked at random and
    imprisoned,
In general, for petty or invented wrongs.

Thus Yoshel, the husband of my mother's sister Hinde,
Found himself slaving in Siberian waters.

From Switzerland, Mother had sent white flour,
And he exchanged it for twice the amount of cheaper rye,
To bake more bread for his large family.
That was his criminal offense.

He was a Titan with a flaming beard, but shy and of few words.
A pious Jew, he would not touch the *treife* fodder served in
    camp,
And starved on turnips, beets, potatoes dug up in frozen fields.
On lucky days he caught a pike or fingerling with his bare hands,
While standing in the river.

Of all the men deported from his village,
He was the only one alive after nine months, sustained by faith
    in God,
And no less, by my father's efforts to rescue him.

For a substantial ransom he finally was freed,
And allowed to leave Russia with his family.

He returned to his *shtetel* a gorilla, wild-eyed, hairy.
Bloated from hunger, cold and fever,
He threw himself upon the chicken on the table,
And fell asleep for twenty hours without waking.

For days he sat in his big rocking-chair,
Silent, streams pouring down his cheeks,
Until he finally broke into howling sobs and prayers,
Thanking his God for freedom and survival.

As soon as he recovered, in 1939, they packed up for the States,
Where, in the meantime, we had gone to live.

Unlike his wife, a real *Misnagid*, Yoshel was a *Chasid*.
To him America meant Brooklyn, where a great *Rebbe* he
    revered,
A famous master of *Chasidim*, lived and ruled.

They settled in the *Rebbe's* radiance,
And he became Yoshel's adviser, guide, and teacher.

In due time Yoshel found work in his field as kosher wine-maker.
But he disliked the mechanized, big factory,
A far cry from his *shtetel*, where he picked grapes,
And trod them barefoot in a tub.
He perked up only, brewing *mead* for *Pesach* in the Rebbe's
    cellar.
That was a special *mitzve* he enjoyed.

Yoshel's rough bulk hid a soft core.
At marriages and funerals he wiped off tears,
Blowing his nose to cover them, too pent up to show feelings.

Alone in synagogue, with his *Chasidim*, he would shed shyness.
Submitting to a mystic bond with God,
He gave himself in fervent chants and prayers,
Oblivious to the world around.

Yet never did he look down on an unbeliever.
Thus he admired and trusted my free-thinking father,
Just pitying him for what he missed.
Yoshel was sure that by including Father in his daily prayers,
He was, in part, responsible for his success in life,
And therefore he accepted his financial help quite naturally.

When he was faced with an important problem,
The choice of schools, physicians, jobs,
He always turned to Father first,
But never followed his advice without the blessings of the *Rebbe*.

Once, doctors recommended surgery for Yoshel's grandson.
The boy's bad limp could be corrected by shortening his longer
     leg.
The *Rebbe* was opposed: "One must not interfere with God's
     creation,
And cut into a healthy limb."
Father called in a *Rebbe* from another town. His verdict was:
"Defective functioning of the body is a sickness.
To cure it, any intervention is allowed."

After long theological discussions under my father's subtle
     guidance,
Both *Rebbes* gave the boy their benediction. The operation was
     a triumph.
On *Purim*, two months later, he danced the *horah* with his
     friends.

In his spare time, Yoshel devoured the Yiddish dailies.
Discarding local politics and gossip,
He only read about the Jews in Palestine and under Hitler.

When finally the State of Israel was proclaimed,
He dreamed of being part of it some day.

This dream was never to come true.
Yoshel died at the age of sixty-nine, dancing in synagogue on
     Simhat Torah.
Entranced and out of breath, the Torah in his arms,
His beard and caftan flying, he suddenly collapsed with a loud
     moan,
An oak struck by a thunder bolt.

To Hinde, death bestowed by God, was to be taken stoically.
This suited her *Misnagid* level-headed nature.
She missed the gently awkward presence of her Yoshel,
Adjusting to widowhood quietly, without tears.

Now she had time to brood about the past.
Hinde was older, and still single, when my mother married.
In order to correct what was considered then a humiliation,
She pruned three years to become Mother's junior.
A privilege she held on to until her dying day.

Yoshel, the first man she had ever dared to look at,
Was introduced to her by the matchmaker of the *shtetel.*
The young man fell in love with her bright smile and auburn
     tresses,
And she melted away under his wooing eyes.

They married and stayed on in Russia, after their relatives had
     left,
Hoping for rights and justice promised by the revolution.
It took but little for them to come down to earth, and no regrets
     to leave.

In time, Hinde, more practical and realistic,
Had learned to hold the reins of Yoshel, her big dreamer,
Lovingly, never disputing his authority.
A willow, swaying and at ease, she smoothed his edges,
Took his *Chasidic* ways into her stride,
While staying true to her own cool, collected self.

Even the grocer in their street held her in awe.
She picked twenty-five items from his shelves, adding up prices
    in her head,
And with a twinkle in her eyes, she quoted the correct amount,
    including taxes,
Before he had a chance to check it on his register.

She always kept her smile, but knew well what she wanted.
In her quiet way, she dominated.
When Yoshel died, she carried on, holding the family together.

Three of their children had already made lives for themselves.
Rachel, the youngest, her two daughters, son, and husband
    remained with Hinde.

Their neighborhood in Brooklyn had deteriorated,
Muggings, thefts, murders threatening everywhere.
One night they chased away a man, about to enter through their
    fire-escape.

Now, more than ever, they yearned to go to Israel,
To help develop and defend the country.

Meanwhile, my mother, after Father died,
Joined Feny, my young sister, in Jerusalem.
She bought herself a flat in Feny's house,
And one for Hinde and Rachel near Tel Aviv.

They cried with joy, and could not wait to leave.
The day of their departure, Hinde came to the airport in her
    Sabbath-best,
Wearing a lace dress and her mother's golden broach and
    earrings.

She had arrived two hours earlier, sat in the lounge,
A dowager holding court, her children, cousins, grandchildren,
All there to see her off. When asked why she got dressed up for
    the trip,
She said indignantly: "Well, don't you understand my child,
I am going to the Holy Land!"

The holy Land received them with a tropical *chamsin*,
And when they reached their flat, scorched, drenched with sweat,
The shower did not work.

But nothing curbed their enthusiasm.
They dropped their luggage, made for the beach, and plunged
    into the sea,
Like a bride into the *mikve* before her wedding night.
They thought of Yoshel in Siberian waters.
Were he still with them, these waves would wash away his
    memories.

For the first time in years, they went to bed with open windows,
Away from Brooklyn's muggers and *ganovim*.
When they awoke, their clothes were scattered on the floor,
All valuables, silver candle-sticks, broach, earrings vanished.
Only the money Hinde hid under her pillow, out of habit, was
    not stolen.

Hinde reigned gently over her family in war-torn Israel.
She only abdicated when my mother came to visit.
Whenever this occurred, there was a feast.
They showered her with love and sweets, and home-made
    delicacies.
Mother disliked the fuss. She was embarrassed.
To her the privilege was to give.
She did it naturally, grateful for joys she sowed and reaped.

When Hinde died three years before my mother, her age,
    officially, was ninety.
Now, side by side, both lie in the most beautiful, idyllic cemetery.
It overlooks the soft hills of Jerusalem,
While smells of pine needles and bay leaves shroud the dead.

---

*temples of kilowatts, from epic poem, ''The Night of Poetry''; treife, not kosher; Misnagid, enlightened Jew; Chasid, pious sect Jew; Rebbe, undisputed leader of a Chasidic sect; mead, wine made of honey; Pesach, Passover; mitzve, meritorious act; Purim, celebration of Jewish deliverance from Haman's plot to kill them (ancient Persia); horah, Jewish national dance; Simhat Torah, day of rejoicing of the Torah; chamsin, hot desert wind; mikve, ritual bath; ganovim, thieves.

I*n the synagogue*

Prayer

Planes from the Holy Land
Leave at unearthly hours.
The *sherut* picks me up at dawn,
Stops for an Arab passenger
At the Old City.
It glows in the sun rising.

Far off, a Bedouin on a mule
Traces his shadow
Along the whitened wall.
A hooded figure flits
Past Jaffa Gate.

Jerusalem asleep,
Tamar and Amnon
Arm in arm,
Stroll round the corner,
The prophet Jeremiah
Passes, stooped in thought.

I ward off visions, feelings
Alien to my agnostic self,
Forces stirring
Under this peaceful panorama.
Here miracles occur.

Unwittingly I pray: "Oh Lord,
Let there be yet another!"

---

*sherut, collective taxi service.

91

In *the cemetery*

La Signora Rossa

"This is where, one day, I'll be buried," Alis said.
I burst out laughing: "You the communist,
You want to lie with orthodox reactionaries!"
"Down there we're all alike," she smiled.
"That's where there is real communism."

The site was Lengnau, in the heart of Switzerland, the year was
     1958.
We had come here with our easels,
And now we sat above the ancient cemetery and sketched its
    tombstones,
Crooked, moss-eaten, some leaning to the back, some forward,
Like Jews in prayer at the wailing wall.

Alis was born in Lengnau thirty years after Jews were allowed
Freedom of residence throughout the country, and equal rights.
Until then, they had lived in Endingen and Lengnau,
Two villages assigned to them.

A few had emigrated earlier.
Meyer Guggenheim went to America in 1848,
And with his sons amassed great fortunes.

But most Swiss Jews took time to leave their ghetto
When the decree opened all doors in 1866.
Many were cattle dealers without professions.
They had no means to move, even within their country.
Their children were more enterprising.
Parched with the thirst for knowledge and adventure,
They poured into the titillating cities.

As soon as Alis finished school, she went to Zürich as a
    seamstress.
Her cat-green eyes, red hair, and long-legged feline stride,
Turned people's heads when she passed by.
She never noticed. She only saw the scene around her,
The glittering city, its displays, elegant people, stores, cafés.
When men approached her, Alis blushed and ran,
A frightened kitten.

One Sunday she installed herself with a small picnic in the park,
And curled up on a bench, she nibbled at her sandwich,
    fondling a book.

"You are reading War and Peace," she heard someone address
    her.
A dark-haired slender man had settled at her side,
Speaking with a strong foreign accent.
"I've read it many times in Russian, my own language," he
    continued.
"If this is your first time, I envy you the experience."

She stared at him wide-eyed.
A Russian here in Switzerland! Why wasn't he at home, fighting
    the war?"

94

Maybe he was a spy, a Bolshevik, a Menshevik.
She had heard these words not knowing what they meant.
The man seemed gentle, though. His smile was warm.
His brown eyes looked at her inquiringly, almost pleading.
He could have been a poet, with his fine chiseled features,
High forehead and expressive hands. This was no man to be
    afraid of.

"Please forgive my intrusion," he said getting up.
"I am alone here, and you looked so 'sympatisch.'
Sorry to have disturbed you."

"I have some grapes," she stopped him. "Would you please
    share them with me?"
Alis was stunned by her own voice.
Never before had she responded to a stranger in the street.

"My name is Sasha," he said smiling. "And I am Alis."
When they shook hands, she knew that something beautiful
    and crucial
Was to change her life.

All afternoon they walked the crooked lanes of the old city.
In a café along the Limmat they had wine and cheese,
And talked until its doors were closing.
From then on, not a day went by without their meeting.

Behind the dormant kitten, Sasha sensed a tigress, passionate
    and strong.
But, not to scare her off, he never made advances.

He grew to be her mentor, gave her books they discussed,
Took her to concerts and museums, and above all,
He taught her the ideas of Engels, Marx, and Rosa Luxemburg,
Explaining the most complicated matters in a clear, simple way.
One day, when Sasha read her Shakespeare's sonnets,
She fell around his neck, the tigress come alive.

Alis moved into his mansard, close to heaven.
Defying all conventions, soaring above clouds, she shared his life,
Though, knowing well, there were some facets that excluded her.

At times, Sasha went off for a few days without an explanation.
Then he returned to her with chocolates, books, a silver pin, a
    ring.
He saw no friends, received no mail at his address,
Went to some "office" every day, always had enough money in
    his purse.

She trusted him and asked no questions,
Convinced he stood for a good cause, for brotherhood and justice.

One afternoon, it was the 7th day of November, 1917,
She heard him jump upstairs, whistling the *Internationale*.
He dashed into the flat, jubilant, out of breath,
Lifted and whirled her through the room with kisses, laughs,
    and cheers.
"Our revolution has succeeded," he proclaimed.
"The Bolsheviks seized power. Long live Lenin!"

Only when he calmed down, did he announce his imminent
    departure.
Alis, dumbfounded, had no words.
He held her in his arms, tried to console her:
"We shall not part for long," he said,
"I cannot live without you, you will join me soon."
He packed, kissed her goodbye, and left a POB address in
    Moscow.

Long letters reassured her of his love,
Advising her, for the time being, not to come.

Alis had grown into a woman, surer of herself, and more mature.
She had a natural flair for style and color,
And found work as assistant to a French designer.
She now wore fashionable clothes, tight dresses to set off her
    figure,
Green hues to stress her eyes.

Men flocked around and wooed her, but she only longed for
    Sasha.
After a year she could bear it no longer.
She sent a telegram to Moscow, announcing her arrival.

Sasha came to the train with a bouquet of roses.
He had lost weight and grown a beard, all salt and pepper.
It made him look much older, and he seemed reserved.
He took her to a room in a small inn behind the station.
Due to the raging civil war, he said, his flat had been destroyed.

They fell into each other's arms.
Alis, exhausted and at peace, slept through the night
In spite of fire alarms and shooting in the street.
But Sasha could not close an eye.
When she awoke, she found him sitting at her side.
He looked at her with such despair, that she got frightened,
And sobbing like a child, he told her he was married.
He had kept quiet, not to upset her, hoping for a divorce before
     she came.
Now his wife Vera threatened suicide if he left her.

When Alis dried her tears, her head was reeling.
She got dressed in a daze, and walked out of the house.
Sasha tried to restrain her, but she pushed him off. She had to
     be alone.

She staggered through the streets of Moscow,
Not hearing bombs or guns around her, a sleep-walker,
     benumbed.
She did not know how long she had been drifting.
Her legs were giving out, and she sat down.

Children were picking through a garbage bin for food.
A little girl approached her, holding out her hand.
And suddenly Alis came back to life.
"These are the homeless war orphans Sasha had talked about,"
     she thought.

Her heart went out to the sad little being.
She reached into her pocket, found a candy, put it into the
     pleading palm.
The little face lit up, and Alis smiled.
She stroked her head and kissed her cheek, all smeared and dirty.

For a long while, they sat together, silent.
Alis had put her arm around her,
And when she looked again, the child was sleeping.
She took off her warm wrap, covered her gently, and slipped
    away.

Looking around she recognized the Kremlin in the distance,
St. Basil's onion domes.
Places and forms resumed their contours and their clarity.
Something in Alis had snapped into place.
She was ashamed of her self-pity.
The night was falling, she found her way to the inn.

Sasha was pacing the room when she entered.
He was beside himself, grabbed her and shook her by the
    shoulders.
"Where have you been," he screamed. "Are you out of your
    mind?
A stranger alone in this seething city!"

Alis had never heard him raise his voice before.
She tried to soothe him with caresses.
He looked so miserable. She was sorry for him.
Now, over the first shock, she realized that he had lied to her
Only to keep her happiness unruffled.

The pain he caused her, she considered a small price
For the rich seeds that he had sown.
He opened up horizons she had never dreamed of,
Unfolded facets of her she did not suspect,
And taught her a new world and way of life.

Now he was trapped, and she had the key to release him.
She sat straight up and held his hand.
"I've made a decision," she said quietly.
"We can't build our happiness on Vera's tomb.
I know you have to stay with her, and I must go.
But I want part of you to go with me."
That night, Alis conceived the fruit of her great love.

When she arrived in Zürich three months later,
Unmarried, with a budding belly, her parents met her at the
    station.
Alis expected them to treat her as an outcast.
They never uttered a reproach. When little Ruth was born,
They took her in and raised her.

There was now one more mouth to feed.
Alis got a new job as buyer for an elegant boutique.

One Sunday she went to the movies by herself,
And saw a film about Rodin, the sculptor, working in his studio.
Spellbound, she sat through three shows.

The following day, during her lunch hour, she bought some clay
    and tools,
And started modelling in her room at night.
Within a year, she had created a whole world.
Voluptuous women and their mates, acrobats, dancers,
Children, owls and rabbits.

She took slides to the curator of the museum.
He came to see her work. Struck by its candor,
The tenderness of her strong, earthy figures,
He offered her an exhibition.

It was the start of a life-long career.
Her work was in demand and shown in galleries,
Critics praised "the new star on the old horizon."
She left her job, and moved to a penthouse studio
With the whole city at her feet.
This called for paint and easel. Alis took to the brush.
Her first attempt was bought and hung in the town-hall.
She was now an established artist, part of the city's Mont
        Parnasse.

Zürich, embodiment of order and stability, had become
        playground
Of an artistic group which cast conventions, rules and logic to
the winds.
These Dadaists, Hulsenbeck, Tsara, Janco, Ball, Hans Richter,
Held court at the Café Voltaire, their literary outlet,
And laughed at the world.
By 1920 they dispersed to Paris and Berlin.

Alis had watched them with amusement.
To her they were not artists, but buffoons.
In spite of her progressive theories she was, at heart, a
        bourgeois cat,
Fond of her niche and downy comforts,
Traditional in taste, respecting her métier.

Her home was warm and hospitable, with pictures on the walls,
Bright pillows strewn invitingly on chairs and rugs.
Friends would drop in, relax over a glass of wine,
Air personal problems, gossip, debate trends, events.

They discussed art for art's sake, social realism,
Gebrauchsmusik composed by Hindemith
For easy use and understanding by the masses,
His shift to difficult atonal music, tabooed by Hitler as *entartete
        Musik*,
And the premiere in Zürich of his opera *Mathis Der Maler*,
At the Swiss National Fair in 1938.
They talked about James Joyce who died in 1941 in Zürich,
The lone wolf, Herman Hesse, in town but never seen,
And Thomas Mann, living in a big house along the lake,
With his wife Katia and six children.

His son and daughter Klaus and Erika had improvised *Die
        Pfeffermuehle*,
A cabaret where biting tongues of refugee comedians
Tore politicians, bureaucrats, and the establishment to shreds.

Many professors, actors, writers,
Had fled across the German border into Switzerland.
It was the only place where they could use their language.
Zürich became their most important center of activity.

Alis' friends, like many intellectuals and artists of that time,
Looked to the Soviet Union for salvation,
And she, the liberated, unwed mother who'd been to Russia,
Was their torchbearer.

Purges of Soviet Jews, rumored atrocities,
As well as Stalin's pact with Hitler, muffled Alis' enthusiasm.
But she blamed Stalin, and not the regime.
"There's no birth without convulsions," she tried to defend her
        cause,
"Russia is still in labor."

Although she never lacked a lap to purr on,
Alis did not forget her first great love.
With World War II, their correspondence stopped completely.
But she still hoped to reunite some day, and have Ruth meet
	her father.
She kept his letters locked, his picture on her desk,
His words engraved within her.

"Only in solitude can we perceive our inner voice and be
	creative,"
Sasha once had said. These words now haunted her.
She felt she had been numbed by city life, its noises and
	distractions.
Her work had lost its freshness. It seemed impersonal and
	shallow.

This struck her like a revelation.
She had to leave, regain her inner core, before it was too late.

Her daughter, Ruth, a gentle faun with Sasha's soft brown eyes,
	unruly curls,
A solid Swiss, with no ambition to redo the world,
Was now a nurse, and married to a pediatrician she adored.
He was eighteen years older, and the father she had longed for.

Ruth was her mother's pal, caring, affectionate,
In spite of their political dissent,
Secure and independent, no more in need of help.
Alis left Zürich freed of obligations, without regrets.
She moved to the quiet, scenic village of Muzzano,
Nestled in the Italian part of Switzerland.

In a neglected old palazzo, she rented a big, sunny room,
With outhouse, a small kitchen, and a den for guests,
And in no time she was at home,
Surrounded by her paintings and belongings.

There was no bathroom, only one cold-water faucet.
But French doors opened on a vine-clad terrace, and steps led
    down a path
Along wild berry bushes, fig and olive trees,
To a small lake where one could bathe and swim.

Of the adjoining patio, Alis made her sculpture garden.
Children climbed its high walls, peeked at its nudes,
And called it "il bordello."

The villagers were proud to have an artist in their midst.
Alis became Muzzano's *castellana*, named "la signora rossa,"
For her political convictions, as much as for the color of her hair.

They called on her for letters to be read or written,
For quarrels to be settled, for advice.

One day, a family from Berne came to live in Muzzano.
Toni, their little boy, had asthma. He needed a mild climate.
The children of the village mocked his accent,
And Gino, their tough leader, kicked and beat the frail
    "tedesco,"
Who always came home crying, with a bleeding nose and blues.
Once, Toni's mother pulled the culprit by his ears into the
    house,
And spanked him with a leather belt.
The boy ran screaming through the streets, she after him,
Fists clenched and calling him "Du miesser Kater."

When Gino's mother rushed to her son's rescue,
Both women jumped at one another, all nails and teeth.
Rolling together in the dust, they pulled each other's hair,
Cursed, screamed, while people stood around the piazza,
Cheering, taking sides.

Alis, who spoke both languages, was called.
With pain she disengaged the furies.
She took each by the arm, and led them to a bench.
They sat for a few moments, bleeding, out of breath.
Then, looking up, they both exploded into laughter.

Alis invited the two women to her house.
She gave them soap and water to wash up, a strong espresso,
And off they went arm in arm.
From that day on, Gino was Toni's bodyguard and friend.

Such happenings were an artistic treat for Alis.
They touched her deeply, and she captured them on canvas,
With humor and humanity.
She often took a sketch-book on her bicycle,
Searched nearby villages for subjects,
Returning loaded with new treasures in the evening.

Sometimes she did not see a soul for weeks, lost in her work.
Her sole companion was Meenoosh, the amber-speckled white
    angora cat.
She worshipped him. But one day he was gone, not to be found.
Alis was inconsolable.

Half a year later, on a winter morning,
She spotted his familiar freckled fur
Around the ponderous shoulders of the butcher's wife.
Snatching it off her, she ran home, tears pouring down her
    cheeks.

That night she could not bear to be alone.
She packed her toothbush and pajamas, and took the bus to
    Zürich.

The Bolshoi ballet toured in town,
And she invited Ruth to go with her.
Everything Russian struck a minor chord in her.
She closed her eyes, and dreamed during the intermission.
The next piece was to be *Petrushka*.
Ruth fingered through the pages of the program,
And with a sudden jerk, she gasped.
Listed among performers, was a ballerina with her father's name.

They could not wait to rush back-stage after the show, to find
    her.
She was no relative. But she knew Sasha from the articles
He wrote for *Pravda*. Alas, not long ago, she read that he had
    died.
He had been ill for many years.
Alis and Ruth staggered out of the theater.
They walked into the night, and talked for hours,
Their hope of ever seeing Sasha gone.
Huddled against each other, they shared their grief.

As her red mane was turning white, people still looked
When Alis passed, a statuesque appearance in home-spun wraps,
Loose tunics she made of exotic fabrics, and comfortable
     espadrilles.

She now turned more and more towards the past,
And often painted childhood scenes from Lengnau:
Her mother lighting candles Friday night,
Jews in the synagogue, dancing around the Torah,
Couples under the bridal canopy, the *huppah*.

These pictures were naïve and pure in style,
Small, intimate, full of nostalgic tenderness.

Alis remained a visionary till the end.
As she had wished, she's buried now in Lengnau.
Her headstone stands erect, a torch,
Among the swaying tombstones
We once sketched.

In *the classroom*

Catacombs

I enter Bet Shearim, third century necropolis in Galilee,
And with a horde of chattering children,
Follow the guide's torch into catacombs
Hewn out of white, calcareous rock.

Chains of high arches, awkward, carved unevenly,
Lead into vaulted burial chambers.
Niches along the walls contain sarcophagi.
Here patriarchs, priests, judges and their families are buried.

As we advance, the halls grow narrow, ceilings, arches low,
The air too heavy to inhale.
I pant and turn my head, somewhat concerned.
Far off, I see the reassuring dot of daylight where we started.

To enter the last hall, one must bend down, creep through.
Inside there is no room to straighten up.
I gasp for air, can't catch my breath, and suddenly
Possessed by unsuppressible mad panic,
I break out like a raging beast.
Pushing aside whoever's in my way,
I scream: "Let me get out, I'm dying!"
The cubicle is full, and yet more children
Crawl like worms through the small hole and block it.

With feet and fists I fight against their forward thrust.
Ready to kill, to crush, to crumble walls,
I run for life towards the dot of light
Beyond the burial chambers.
Their vaults reverberate my primal scream.

The ritual slaughterer

Rivkah

She was a prisoner tied to the bed,
Tubes in her arm, helpless with heat and pain.

A morphine shot had given her wings.
Relieved and in a trance, she tore the tubing from her veins,
Threw off her gown and, unaware of nakedness,
Wandered about the ward from bed to bed.
Caressing patients in their sleep,
She whispered solaces to them in the Hungarian dialect
She had not spoken since her childhood.

A man sat up quite startled. This was his mother tongue.
"Who are you? What are you doing here?" he asked.
"I am the rabbi's daughter,"Rivkah told him. "I make the
        rounds
To help the inmates of the camp. That is my mission.
You see," she added, "a Nazi shot my husband
When he jumped the train to Bergen Belsen.
I hid our children, six of them, with Father Benedict,
And stayed alone with Rochale, my baby.
The S.S. picked us up right off the street,
And dragged us here to Buchenwald."

The man dressed a large towel around her.
His heart was heaving with compassion.
"You are in Israel, my dear," he whispered gently.
"Hitler died forty years ago. There's no more Buchenwald.
This is the Haifa hospital."

"No, no," she muttered, "This is Buchenwald. Don't talk so
    loud.
If Horst should find me here, he'll kill you.
He's jealous. I'm his property.
He put me in the kitchen as their cook.
Thank God for that. This way I can hide food
For Rochale and others in the camp.
I must survive, you understand,
For the sake of my children and those who need help."

She looked around. "I am so scared of him," she whispered.
"Each time he touches me, I close my eyes and let him do his
    dirty thing,
While I recite the *Sh'ma* and numb my senses.
Sometimes, may God forgive me, I forget myself and feel a spark
    of pleasure.
Then I'm afire with shame and with remorse.
Imagine me, a Jew, in the arms of a Nazi!"
She stopped and looked at him.
"You are the first person I've told this to," she said.

The stranger gently took her hand and kissed it.
"Thank you for telling me" he murmured, and his voice was
    choking.
"You are a saint and a great lady. You have nothing to hide.
I hope we will be friends when we get out of here."

He rang the nurse to help her back to bed.
That night she fell asleep and did not wake again.

Sh'ma, Jewish daily prayer, recited also facing death.

The water carrier

Birds

Toybale was the younger of two sisters and the pretty one.
She was not the tame dove her name suggested.
A lively lark, she liked to spread her wings,
Sing, laugh, play impish games.

Longing for independence, she studied to become a nurse.
But her real passion was the theater.
Her parents were appalled.
A woman on the stage was a disgrace, a harlot.

This was of no concern to Toybale.
She entered Stanislavski's competition secretly
And won a scholarship.

Three nights a week, floating on clouds,
She went to drama school, pretending nursing duties,
Until, one day, her name appeared in a review
Praising the school's performance of the "Sea Gull."

Her father read the paper and exploded.
Sea gull and lark had to come down to earth.

Meanwhile the Russian civil war was raging.
All vacant rooms were seized by the Red Army.
Forestalling an invasion of their home,
Toybale's parents promptly offered their free den
To a young Jewish doctor she had met at work.

Hirshel was hounded and half-crazed.
Bolsheviks shot his father in his presence.
Too ready to console him,
Toybale found herself with child.

Her father, barely over his first shock,
Now had to face another scandal.

Immediate marriage was his only answer.
A younger daughter, though, could not be led to the altar,
Unless the older one was married off as well.
Such were the customs of the time,
Regardless of upheavals, wars, and revolutions.

A dowry was offered for the older sister,
Matchmakers came flocking with their grooms,
Two weddings soon restored the honor of the clan.

Toybale bore a cherub, blond and curly,
Named after Hirshel's father Velve.

When guns and cannons finally were silenced,
The family moved from Kiev to Geneva.
Thanks to the fortune left abroad by his late father,
Hirshel established a new practice.

Lancing a patient's abcess, he threw up and fainted.
Toybale came to the rescue as his nurse.
Since he had witnessed his own father's execution,
Hirshel could no longer bear the sight of blood.
His short-lived medical career thus ran its course.

So did his short-lived life, when at the age of thirty,
Struck by blazing fever, he burned out.

Widowhood was not for Toybale. She shed some genuine tears,
Her golden skin set off becomingly by black,
Then cheerfulness took over.

Her life revolved around her son.
Throughout his pre-school years he was her doll.
She showed off his long locks,
Took him to Monte Carlo, Cannes, St. Moritz.
Exposed to beauty contests, he won prizes.

When later he attended boarding school in England,
Toybale camped nearby and shared his world,
At ease among the upper classes of society.

Europe's disruption in the thirties,
Chased them across the ocean to New York.

There Toybale became Tatiana and Velve Vania, à la Chekhov.
A modest "de" preceding their last name,
Established them as Franco-Russian aristocracy,
And lent new wings to their ascension.
This self-appointed delicate promotion
Called for a certain way of life.

Tatiana took up residence in a quiet Tudor City flat,
Furnished with Louis quinze tête-à-têtes,
Prints by François Boucher and Fragonard.

She soon became a favorite hostess of New York's café society.
Dorothy Thompson, Elsa Maxwell, Dali, Marlene Dietrich,
As well as lesser luminaries, lawyers, writers, politicians,
Were honored to be asked to the salon
Of this most gracious Russian noblewoman.
House concerts were offered with vodka and sakuskis,
And one could count on stimulating conversations and
    encounters.

A crown of her blond tresses
Wound around the head in "Gretchen" fashion,
And always in a navy Chanel suit offset by pearls,
Tatiana played her part convincingly,
With little intermissions here and there.

When corsets got too tight, she fled to Flatbush
To relax in Yiddish with her sister,
Catch up on family gossip and gefillte fish.

Vania studied law at Princeton.
He had to cope with problems of identity.
Psychoanalysis turned him against his mother,
Discharging deep-rooted resentments.
To break loose from her loving clutches, he refused to see her.
Even his graduation she could not attend.
Later, as international lawyer, he asked
To be transferred to Hong Kong, out of reach.

Tatiana lived alone, with parties, concerts, theaters,
And charities to keep her busy.

For years she had a passionate affair with a Canadian senator.
His wife was paralyzed, and he could not desert her.
Tatiana was his lover, friend and confidante.
She shared his worries faithfully and with compassion.
His visits to New York were his escape into her warm, exotic
    world.

But gradually her role as orchid in the dark
Lost glamour and attraction.
Passion wore off and other lovers found their way
To her big heart, their haven from reality,
While she was dreaming of a gentle eagle
To shelter her under his wings.

The bird who flew into her nest one night,
Swinging a silver-headed cane,
An elder gentleman with greetings from a friend in Paris,
Was a French baron straight off a canvas by Toulouse Lautrec.
Tall, elegant, in striped grey trousers, top-hat,
Monocle, gloves, spats, he wore in his lapel a red carnation,
And a pink pearl pinned to his pale-slate tie.

Tatiana, young at seventy, thanks to plastic patch-work,
In her white hostess gown bedecked with gold,
Sang Russian gypsy songs with a dark, mellowed voice,
To friends assembled for some borscht and piroshkis.

The baron was bewitched. He lingered after everyone was gone.
All night they laughed and talked like cronies.
They baptized their new friendship with champagne,
Had breakfast overlooking Brooklyn's skyline,
Watched tug-boats on the river and the sunrise.
By morning lark and eagle had turned into turtle-doves.

Tatiana and André became inseparable.
He spoiled and worshipped her
With "trifles" by Cartier, poems and "billets doux,"
Red roses at her door-step every morning.

André kept a suite at the Ritz in Paris.
When they arrived on the first day of May,
White lilies of the valley in their rooms
Fanned out a fragrant welcome.

A civil marriage sealed their union,
Solemnized Chez Maxim with caviar and "Veuve Cliquot."
Tatiana now was a legitimate "baronne."
Using her husband's coat of arms as letterhead,
She did not waste a day to spread the word.

To André Paris was his castle. He took Tatiana on a tour.
They cruised by "bateau mouche" along the Seine,
Explored the flea market, its "bal musette,"
Had bouillabaisse at the Bistro des Halles.
They saw Molière's "Les Femmes Savantes,"
Went up the Eiffel Tower and down to "Mona Lisa" at the
    Louvre.

André adored showing his country to Tatiana,
Gliding along the tree-lined lanes built by Napoleon.
They visited "chateaux" on the Loire, cave drawings at Lascaux,
Stopped on the way to see his friend Josephine Baker.
She owned a medieval village in Dordogne,
Complete with church and castle, four star inn,
And race tracks, to sustain her nine adopted children.

In Valoris they picked up pottery from Picasso.
They lunched with Chagall at St. Paul's "Colombe d'Or."

Picasso, Braque, Léger, when still unknown, had painted there,
And paid for meals with canvasses now on the walls.

Tatiana and André spent winters in New York or Paris,
Nestling at home with music, books, and friends.
Their honeymoon continued through the years.
Aware of blessings, they savored every moment.

One day at breakfast in their Tudor City flat,
Tatiana felt a penetrating pain. She could not catch her breath,
And with a gasping shriek, she suddenly collapsed.

It was a massive heart attack.
The doctors gave no hope.
André was horrified and did not leave her side.
He held her hand, tears running down his cheeks.

For a few minutes she came to and smiled at him,
As if apologizing for the pain she caused.
She knew her time was up.

"I want to tell you something I have kept from you" she
    mumbled.
"Don't talk my dear" he hushed her, "I know everything.
You are my Jewish queen, I sensed it ever since we met.
How charmingly you played your part!
I loved you even more for it."
"You know," he added, "I too have a confession.
My grandmother slipped with her banker, Mr. Cohn,
And I am his descendent." He kissed her hand,
"You see, we are birds of a feather."

She chuckled faintly, a slight twinkle in her eyes.
"Oh, what a farce!" she whispered, and was gone.

Sanctification

"C'e Piu Tempo Che Vita"

She dozes in her rocking chair,
Browsing through memories.

Most of her friends have reached beyond.
She sees them in her sleep,
At ease with their familiar faces,
Ready to join them, and in turn,
To visit dreams of those still chasing time.

The phone rings: "Grandma, are you well?"
"Yes darling, just a little lonely.
You haven't been here for so long."
"I miss you too. Time flies, and I'm so busy.
Maybe next week I'll come to see you."

She puts down the receiver.
Shutting her eyes, she returns to her ghosts.
Their time stands still. They never fail her.

_____

Italian proverb: "There's More Time Than Life"

The glazier

The matchmaker